LEATHER
Jewelry

LEATHER
Jewelry

35 beautiful step-by-step leather accessories

Linda Peterson

CICO BOOKS
LONDON NEW YORK

Dedication:
I would like to dedicate this book to my son Alex.
I am so proud of you and the great husband and father
you have become. I love you with all my heart!

Published in 2015 by CICO Books
An imprint of Ryland Peters & Small Ltd
20–21 Jockey's Fields
London WC1R 4BW
341 E 116th St
New York NY 10029

www.rylandpeters.com

10 9 8 7 6 5 4 3 2 1

Text © Linda Peterson 2015
Design and photography © CICO Books 2015

A CIP catalog record for this book is available
from the Library of Congress and the British
Library.

ISBN: 978 1 78249 245 0
Printed in China

Editor: Marie Clayton
Designer: Mark Latter
Step-by-step photography: Geoff Dann
Style photography: Emma Mitchell
Styling and art direction: Luis Peral
Template illustrations: Stephen Dew

contents

introduction

I have just diagnosed myself with ADCD—that is Attention Deficit Creative Disorder, to which I hope there is no cure in sight! Its symptoms include an insatiable desire to create beautiful things with all sorts of different materials, as well as a debilitating hatred associated with housework and other domestic duties. It's hard for me to focus on just one genre or medium, because there are so many things to make! Given that though, jewelry making ranks high on my list of passions.

In all seriousness though, I am a born craftinista. I've always been creative, but it's been an ongoing progress through the years. I create for several reasons: I have to…it's in my soul, but also because I just can't bear to spend money on designer looks when I can make it for less and spend the money I saved on more craft supplies!

I love making jewelry because it's really a statement about your character and who you are as a person. I have a large—or so I'm told—personality and it stands to reason that I like to wear big, bold, statement pieces. I like bright colors, unusual designs, and lots of bling. My Mom, she liked to wear things a little more dainty; she was definitely a proper lady, who was warm, kind, and humble. You could see it by the way she dressed and the jewelry she wore. Given that everyone has different styles, I designed the projects in this book to reflect a variety of personalities.

I love expanding my knowledge of materials and incorporating those into my jewelry making. Among my recent passions in the last few years is working with leather. At first, I tended to shy away from it because it seemed a bit intimidating to work with. But after gathering a few tools and combining them with some of the things I had in my studio, I realized just how wrong I was. The colors, patterns, and textures available in leather today open up a whole new world in jewelry making.

This book is not a complete Bible on everything there is to know about working with leather. Nor will you find that I am a purist; I take on a more mixed media, "anything goes" approach, which you see reflected in the pages of this book. What you will find are designs and projects that you can make successfully—even if it's your first time making your own jewelry or it's your first time working with leather. I've used tools that you most likely already have and kept the specialty tools to a minimum. That said though, it is nice every once in a while to splurge on a quality tool that makes the whole experience more enjoyable. So you may want to invest in a rotary punch and rivet setters. They are relatively inexpensive and I think you'll find that you can use them for way more than just making leather jewelry too.

I spent hours and hours in the studio just playing with techniques, discovering what works and what doesn't, and I encourage you to give yourself some creative play time and do the same. Don't be afraid to paint, mark, glue, sew, scratch, dent, punch holes, or anything else you think might add interest to your work. Don't be afraid to mess up, and think creatively on how to fix it when you do! These are the ways that you expand your knowledge and creativity. Make sure you have lots of flop-portunities!

Begin your leather jewelry journey by creating something simple such as the Purple Waterfall necklace on page 46; it only uses a few materials. Then maybe increase your skillset and learn to set rivets and brads to create some awesome boot bling as in the project on page 106 to turn your ordinary footwear into designer extra-ordinary boots! You'll definitely find the techniques section of the book useful because this outlines some of my favorite techniques that I use multiple times in the projects. So make sure you familiarize yourself with this chapter in particular.

You will also notice that many designs in the book are mix-n-match. This means that you can mix colors or textures from one project with the style of another. Or you can create a base piece of jewelry and easily switch out the focal pieces. In no time you'll be mixing and matching your way into creating your own unique designs and your family and friends will be in awe.

I'm so glad we are taking this journey together, and if you need a little extra advice, don't hesitate to contact me via my email address (see page 126). You can also connect with me on my YouTube channel where
I share helpful hints and jewelry-making tutorials.

Enjoy the journey!

a little bit about leather...

Using leather for all sorts of things goes way back in time; hunters who caught wild animals for food discovered that the hides and skins were useful for creating garments, footwear, and tent making—and much is the same today. However, the uses of leather have increased; it is now used to bind books, cover furniture, make saddles, and for fashion items, and is produced in a wide variety of colors and styles.

The principal method of making leather hasn't changed much since early history. It is an interesting technique, though, and there is loads of historical information on the Internet if you care to search this topic. Since making leather itself is beyond the scope of this book, I won't spend time explaining all the different types and processes. For the most part, I just picked leather that looked and felt good to me. This is important because the leather will be up next to our skin and we want it to be comfortable.

The leather that we will be using for making jewelry is this book is mostly made from cow and deer skins, which makes it easy to obtain and affordable. It comes in a variety of patterns, colors, and textures to suit almost any project. I like the suede and nubuck type of leather, which comes from the inner layer of skin and tends to have a more velvety surface. This type of leather also produces a crisp look when stamping designs onto the leather itself.

Chrome-tanned leather is made with a process that uses chromium sulfate to create a leather that does not discolor or lose its shape and is soft and supple. It accounts for nearly 80% of the leathers produced in the world. You don't really need to know this—there's no test at the end of the book—it's just a fun fact and gives you an idea of the difference between softer leather and harder leather. It's the type of leather I've used in many of the projects in this book.

Vegetable-tanned leather uses tannin, which is found naturally in vegetable matter, in its tanning process. Generally this produces leather that is stiff and usually brown in color.

This type of leather makes great wristbands and is suitable for carving and stamping designs into. In general, if you are purchasing veg-leather in flat skin, chose a 3–4 oz. (85–110 g) weight—this will be suitable for most of the veg-tanned leather projects in the book.

Because we are only using small sections of leather, you can purchase higher quality leather at a more affordable price. And here's a big hint: Check out the scrap bin as buying oddments for small projects can add up to significant savings. Because leather is a natural product, expect it to have some imperfections and variations. For me, I particularly like this aspect as I think it lends a one-of-a-kind touch to my pieces.

Avoid getting your leather wet but if you do, let it dry slowly and naturally. Do not apply heat. If you need to clean a piece, use only products designed to clean leather such as saddle soap, and test on an inconspicuous area first.

Now dive in… it's time to have fun!

designing jewelry

Everybody wants to look their best most of the time, and it's also natural that we tend to wear what we like and what we feel most comfortable in. But consider for just a minute how selecting the right jewelry for your fashion style and individual taste reflects on your confidence level, self-esteem, and overall mood.

How do you feel when your hair and make-up are perfect and you are dressed to the hilt; you are ready to take on what the day will bring. For me, this is empowering! It lifts my self-esteem and confidence level to the "I can do anything I set my mind to do today" mood. In contrast, if I wear no make up and put on my most comfy clothes, my mood goes from "I can do anything" to "...okay, maybe I'll do something" and I'm much less likely to accomplish all that I set out to do.

The way you present yourself, including the accessories that you choose, also says a lot about yourself—especially to others. I'm not for a moment saying that designing jewelry has to be difficult or that you have to put this huge thought process into it every time, but here are some ideas that you might float around in your head while you are involved in the creative process.

A style of jewelry to fit the occasion
If you were attending a very formal wedding, funky, wild jewelry would probably not go very well with a classic, sophisticated dress. Perhaps that is rather a drastic example, but you get the idea: a formal event requires sophisticated and classic jewelry. On the other hand, you wouldn't want to wear tiny, discreet items of jewelry with a colorful and extravagant outfit— on this occasion it would be more appropriate to have big, bold accessories. So, fit the style of jewelry to the occasion.

Deciding what suits you
As I mentioned before, you will feel more comfortable if you wear what you like. Personally I wear mostly my own handmade jewelry: it's bold, sometimes rather chunky, and it's out there—but then again, that's who I am. So now let's talk about creating jewelry that suits who you are. Stop reading for a second and go get a mirror. Hold it up and take a good look at; get up close and personal. Pull your hair back and concentrate on the shape of your face. Let's talk about these different facial shapes and how jewelry can complement them to make you look your very best. A rule of thumb is to select necklines and accessories that are the opposite of your facial shape.

A few of the most common face shapes

Round faces have an equal distance all around the face, with the nose being the center point of measure. This shape is wide with rounded edges, so it is important to add some visual length. Scoop, square, V-neck, or mock turtlenecks are the most complimentary necklines, but stay away from anything that adds visual thickness to your neck. When it comes to jewelry, choose a longer necklace length and pair with oblong or rectangular earrings to create balance.

Oval or Oblong-shaped faces are longer than they are wide. While they look very similar overall, if you were to place them side-by-side, you would be able to see the difference; the oval has soft, rounded curves all round while the oblong is rounded but more angular. Almost any shape of neckline will be flattering to these shape faces, and you have the most options when choosing necklace lengths. You also have the widest choice of jewelry styles, but try adding contrast to an oval shape by wearing angular shapes—and with an oblong face, chokers especially well.

Square or Rectangular facial shapes are very similar, with straight lines at the forehead and down the sides, and a square-shaped chin. The rectangular face is slightly elongated and narrower, but both of these shapes have strong, defined lines. Choose necklines such as turtlenecks, jewel necks, or those that hang off the shoulder, to soften the angular effect. With jewelry, shapes that are round and wide are best and consider longer earrings to soften a strong jaw line. If your face is narrower, short dangling earrings can help fill out the sides. With necklaces, try for soft U-shapes and multi-strands to help offset pronounced facial features.

Heart-shaped faces are wider at the eye line and narrow down to the chin, usually with soft lines and curves. Scoop and boat-shape necklines work well, but avoid anything that ends in a point such as a V-neck. To balance this shape with jewelry, consider earrings that are the direct opposite, such as triangles that are pointed at the top and wide at the bottom. Chokers, U-shape, or multi-strand necklaces will soften and minimize the point of the chin.

tools and techniques

tools and materials

Nothing is fun if it's not easy! I have tried my best to use tools and materials that are easily sourced; most likely you have many of these items already. I've also tried to keep the specialty tools to a minimum and give you some alternatives when possible. Don't feel that you need to rush out and buy all the tools here before making the projects. Get a feel for which projects and techniques you like the best and then begin by purchasing tools related to them. It's nice to splurge once in a while and a new tool is great for creativity!

Cutting tools

Duckbill scissors are very sharp, inexpensive, and easy to source. They are great for beginners. Once you've grown accustomed to working with leather, invest in a quality pair of leather scissors. These will slice through leather like butter, making cutting of shapes quick and easy. They can also be re-sharpened when needed.

The utility knife is very sharp and is useful in cutting thick leather; use it with a metal rule and a cutting mat to cut perfectly straight lines.

duckbill
scissors

leather
scissors

utility
knife

snips

round-nose
pliers

needle-nose
pliers

Pliers

Needle-nose pliers are all-purpose for use with metal and wire, to open and close jump rings, and to grip small objects. The jaws may have teeth, so be careful that these do not leave marks on the material. Snips are used for cutting wire. I also find them handy to snip off small pieces of excess leather close to the surface. Round-nose pliers are used to curve wire or head pins into a ring,

Hammering tools

The poly mallet has a yellow polymer head for minimal bounce when stamping and punching. It also won't damage your other tools. The metal hammer is good when you need a more powerful blow to punch out a hole. Bench blocks come in different materials; hard for setting eyelets or with a surface that has more give.

poly mallet

bench block

metal head hammer

rubber block

Punching and stamping tools

various metal stamps for creating designs in leather

embossing wheel for making an embossed decorative line

designs created by the punching/stamping tools shown right

A poly block offers the best cutting surface to prolong the life of your punches, chisels, and other cutting tools.

Punches

Used to punch out holes for eyelets, rivets, conchos, or stitching, punches come in a variety of shapes and sizes. There are also special ones for specific uses.

adjustable 2-prong brad punch

4-prong lacing chisel

various size hole punches

round strap end punch

rotary punch

Setting tools

Each setting tool fits a specific hole in the setting block to suit different sizes of eyelet or rivet. It is important to use the correct size setting hole with the eyelet or rivet you are working with.

selection of eyelets and rivets

setting tools

setting block

Coloring tools

There are products specifically designed to colorize leather. However, being the mixed media artist that I am, I like to push the boundaries and experiment with products I have in the studio such as alcohol-based inks, acrylic craft paints, and markers. Have a look around and get creative when looking for products that could be used to color or alter the surface of the leather. Set some time aside for creative play and discovery!

cosmetic sponges, paintbrushes

alcohol-based ink pens

acrylic leather paint

leather dye

antiquing leather stain

basic acrylic craft paints

un-mounted rubber stamps

Rubber stamping tools

Rubber stamps can be used to create many interesting designs when applied to the surface of the leather.

stamping pad

refill ink

detail of the line marks made by the wheeled punch

Sewing tools

I find that the sewing awl, used for saddle-stitching (see page 28), is one of my must-have tools. It is relatively inexpensive but will save stress on your hands when stitching leather. The needle can be stored inside the handle when not in use. The wheeled punch shown next to it will make a line of evenly-spaced marks to use as a stitching guide.

waxed thread

clear silicone-based adhesive

Mod Podge

sewing awl

wheeled punch

Adhesives

There are many different types of adhesive and it's important to choose the correct one for the material and project. Silicone-based adhesive is used for most of the projects where you need to attach an embellishment. Tacky glue is useful to add small items or seal ends, while Mod Podge is mainly used for decoupage.

tacky glues

fibercraft cement

Leather

Upcycled and recycled leather can be found at yard sales, thrift stores, or even in your closet! Give your worn-out ball gloves, handbags, purses, and even boots a new life and make them into something.

Purchased leather is available in a variety of different patterns, textures, and colors. Creating smaller projects like jewelry means you can often work with a quality leather without spending a lot of money.

Leather cords and laces are great to use for knotting techniques and for basic necklaces. They come in a variety of colors and can be round or flat.

braided lacing and round laces

flat laces

Pre-cut leather shapes are a good and inexpensive alternative when you want to create quick leather jewelry pieces. They are generally made of veg-tan leather, which can be colored and textured using a variety of techniques. The leather wristbands are available with or without snaps.

Waxed thread is available in a variety of colors and is used to stitch leather pieces together. It also comes on a spool.

Lace trims

These are another staple in my studio. I like to combine them with other materials when I want to add a soft touch to my projects. Lace gives an instant vintage, shabby chic appearance to my designs and I especially like this look when creating pouches and handbags.

Ribbons

Always a staple supply in my studio. Keep a variety of ribbons with different colors, patterns, and widths handy at all times—they can be used as decorative elements or to create the necklace cords. While they are not leather, they do add an element of interest to your jewelry designs.

findings

General findings

These basic findings are staples in the studio. While I haven't used all of the items shown here, the photo gives you a general idea of the types of findings available for jewelry making.

headpins

ribbon ends

bead caps

cone ends

spacer beads

filigree bead caps

earring wires

ring blanks

jump rings

lobster clasp

Fastenings

These findings are slightly more specialized for leatherwork, although they can be used in other projects too. Though I've not used all the fasteners shown here, these are ones that are the most common.

selection of rivets

snap

magnetic cord

hooks and loops

decorative toggle clasp

spiked button studs

various screw

magnetic clasp

cord

cord ends with extension chains

Brads

Decorative brads come in all finishes, shapes, and sizes. They can really add a nice decorative touch to your projects and are easy to work with.

Chain

A small selection of the many different types of chain available. In this book I've used chain primarily as an embellishment rather than as the basis of a necklace or bracelet, so small decorative bits of chain work well and are good to have on hand.

Buckles and clips

These can be plain and simple or highly decorative. Choose the one that fits in with the rest of your project, or choose a contrasting one as a focal point.

Decorative findings

There are so many decorative findings available that it's impossible to show everything, but here's a selection of my favorites. Some of them are designed for leather and have screw posts while others are simply charms or focal pieces. You don't always need to buy decorative bits—look for broken jewelry at yard sales that you can recycle, or items from hardware stores that can be put to a new use.

Beads

Again just a small selection of the many, many different beads that are available, in so many materials, colors, and shapes. You can't go wrong adding beads and bling to your projects and I keep a generous stash in my studio at all times.

techniques

In this section, you'll find the techniques that I've used over and over again in different projects outlined here for easy reference. When they are needed in a project, a cross-reference will bring you to the correct page in this section. Additional techniques specific to a particular project are detailed within that project.

Cutting

Whatever you are making, you are almost certain to need to cut the leather. There are several ways to do this—which one you choose will depend on the shape you want to create and the thickness of the leather.

Cutting with scissors

Heavy-duty leather scissors will cut most leather; use them just like normal scissors. Duckbill scissors are also good and may be easier to find.

Cutting with a utility knife

On heavier leather or if you need to cut straight lines, use a utility knife and a steel rule. Remember to protect your work surface with a cutting mat. Also, ensure that your fingers are out of the way!

Cutting a hole with a punch

Holes and other shapes can be cut out with a craft punch. There are many of these available—circles in different sizes, half circles, ovals, and other shapes.

1 Place the leather onto a poly board and align the punch where desired. Give it a firm strike with the hammer.

2 Remove the punch to reveal the hole or cut-out shape in the leather.

Tip: When punching the holes, make sure to stand the punch straight up and strike with a firm hit. This will ensure a clean cut.

Setting an eyelet

1 Place the leather on a bench block and punch out a hole corresponding to the size of the eyelet. Push the stem of the eyelet through the hole from front to back.

2 Place the piece on a bench block with the back facing up. Place the end of an eyelet setter in the center of the eyelet stem and hammer firmly—this pushes the eyelet flanges outward to secure it around the hole.

3 Flatten the eyelet with a tap from the hammer.

Tip: When setting decorative rivets, place a scrap of leather in the hole of the setting block to protect the decorative side from damage.

Setting rivets

Generally rivets have two pieces—a front that is sometimes decorative and a plain back side.

1 Place the leather on a bench block and punch out a suitable size hole. Push the stem of the rivet through the hole from front to back. Attach the rivet back on the reverse.

2 Set the rivet into the correct size hole in the rivet setting block.

3 Place the end of the rivet setter in the center of the rivet and hammer firmly to secure it around the hole.

Tip: Rivets come with different stem lengths. You want just enough stem sticking above the leather; too much stem length can cause the rivet stems to bend over and prevent you from achieving a good set.

adding texture

Adding texture is a great way to vary the same piece of leather for different projects. There are several techniques, but here are the two we use in this book.

Stamping

1 Spritz vegetable-tanned leather with water before stamping to soften it and enable it to take a pattern.

2 Place the stamp firmly against leather and then give it a sharp tap with a hammer to emboss the design. Be careful not to move the stamp or hit it more than once because that may blur the outlines.

Embossing

To create texture or a design over larger areas, place the leather inside an embossing folder typically used for embossing paper.

Pass the folder through a pasta machine, set on the thickest setting, by turning the crank. You'll find this is an easy way to create unique patterns onto leather.

Tip: Embossing and die cut machines are available to emboss leather, but they can be expensive. Embossing folders and plates are relatively inexpensive and can be used in a pasta machine, provided that they and the leather are not too thick.

coloring

Sometimes you may be unable to find leather in the shade you want, but coloring it is a good option. You can color just a small area or the whole piece. Here are some of my favorite ways to tint leather.

1 Sponge a little leather dye over the surface of the leather using a cosmetic sponge. Allow to dry completely. The dye tends to sink into the leather itself and is permanent.

2 Use alcohol-based markers to color small areas of leather. This is a great choice if you have stamped a pattern onto the surface of the leather and you want to add some color details.

3 Another option is to paint on the leather using acrylic paint. It's best to build up a design in layers, starting with the lightest color first.

4 On embossed leather you can also wipe over the design with a darker color and then wipe it away while the paint is still wet. The darker color stays in the embossing to highlight the design.

stitching leather

You can sew leather with a sturdy needle and thread, but a stitching awl will make it much easier and you will need one for saddlestitching. You can also join two edges with lacing in cord or ribbon.

Saddlestitching

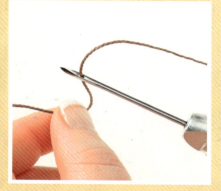

1 Make sure that the groove on the needle is facing you. Thread the needle in the awl from front to back.

2 Place the layers of leather you wish to stitch on a poly block and position the lacing chisel into place.

3 Punch a line of holes with a firm tap of the hammer. To achieve the correct spacing when creating a line of stitching holes, align the first chisel prong into the last hole created each time, and then tap with the hammer. Continue punching as many stitching holes as needed.

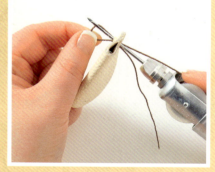

4 Push the needle through the first stitching hole from front to back.

5 Pull the thread end all the way out to the back.

6 Pull the needle tip out of the hole, leaving the thread end in place on the back. Move the needle over one stitch and push the needle through this hole from front to back.

7 Pull back on the needle by about ¼ in. (5 mm) to create a loop of thread and then feed the end of the thread through the loop.

8 Pull the needle back out, and pull gently on the thread and the thread end to secure the stitch. Repeat steps 6 to 8 to the end.

9 To secure the last stitch, press the needle into the hole, then pull up on the needle thread to create a large loop and snip off, leaving two ends

10 Tie the two ends securely in a knot. Trim the ends close to the knot.

Whipstitching   Blanket stitch   Lacing

Punch the stitching holes along near the edge to be whipped. Thread the leather needle, knot the thread end and secure it between layers. Stitch through the holes from back to front each time to whip over the edge.

Punch the stitching holes. Thread the needle and knot the thread end. Bring the needle from back to front through the first hole, then over the edge and up through the next hole from back to front, leaving a loop over the edge. Take the needle down through the loop, ready to come up from back to front through the next hole to make the next stitch. Repeat all the way along and then knot the end to secure.

Punch the stitching holes, or set the eyelets, in matching positions along the two edges. Thread the two ends of the cord or ribbon down the first two holes from front to back. Cross the ends over and bring them up the next pair of holes from back to front. Repeat along the edges. At the finish, tie the two ends into a bow.

Tip: Try out different lacing patterns to get the effect you want—check out trainers or other laced shoes for some creative ideas.

Opening and closing jump rings

Use this simple method to open and close jump rings so you can use them to attach items together.

1 To open the jump ring, hold a pair of pliers on each side of the join and twist the pliers slightly in opposite directions to open up a gap.

2 To close the ring, repeat the twisting action in reverse to bring the two ends back together neatly.

Tip: Don't open a jump ring by pulling the ends apart, because this will distort the shape and it will be hard to get it back into a perfect circle.

Barrel knot

This is a really useful knot to secure a clasp or join two lengths together. It's easier to work with a longer cord even if you need a smaller knot. Cut a length of cord around 10–12 in. (25–30 cm) minimum—longer if you want more wraps.

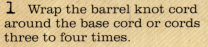

1 Wrap the barrel knot cord around the base cord or cords three to four times.

2 Thread the left end through the loops and out to the right. Thread the right end through the loops and out to the left.

3 Gently pull on both cord ends to tighten the knot. If you are using the knot to attach a clasp, make sure it is positioned tightly against the clasp before tightening the knot.

Making a dangle

Use a headpin and a selection of beads to make your own decorative dangles.

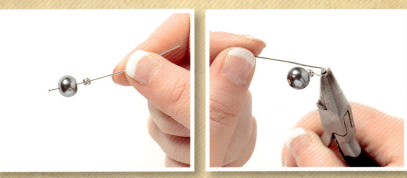

1 Thread the chosen bead or beads and spacer beads onto a headpin.

2 Use round-nose jewelry pliers to curl the top of the headpin into a loop, centering the loop over the beads. Cut off the excess headpin with wire cutters.

chapter 1

make it
simple

hippy-dippy

Celebrate sixties style with this charming pendant that any flower child would have been proud to own.

1 Stamp the shell design (see page 26) all around the edge of the flower motif.

2 Stamp a tiny flower into each scallop. Paint the flower orange, then tip the edges with the red marker. Punch a small hole in one of the shells and use a jump ring (see page 30) to add the leaf dangle to the bottom of the flower.

3 Paint the larger washer white and the smaller one turquoise. Stack the smaller on the larger and then glue the watch winder in the center. Glue onto the center of the flower.

4 Make a triple strand leather lace necklace as explained on page 46. Punch a small hole at the top of the flower, add a large jump ring and thread this onto the necklace.

Tip: One of my washers was already painted white and had an interesting patina. Don't be afraid to reuse old parts, not everything has to be new and shiny.

joyful heart pendant

I like to use heart motifs and spread the love! This necklace is based on a few simple techniques, but building up many layers creates a rich and sumptuous effect.

1 Basecoat the heart in white, then sponge on a mixture of blue and green. Mix the two together slightly as you sponge to create a mottled effect.

2 Paint a smaller red heart on top, slightly off center. Let dry. Stamp over the top of everything with the text stamp.

3 Add a few dots to the red heart with white paint and a toothpick. Outline the main heart with the gel pen and add a few doodles. Glue on a scrap of paper with a word of your choice. Punch a hole at the top of one side of the heart and add a jump ring so it will hang at an angle.

YOU WILL NEED

* Pre-cut leather heart
* Acrylic paint in white, blue, green, and red
* Black inkpad
* Black leather lacing
* Rubber text stamp
* Cosmetic sponge
* Paintbrush
* Toothpick
* Gel ink pen in black
* Scrap of paper
* Glue
* Punch
* Jump ring
* Pliers
* Leather stain

4 I sponged a little stain onto the heart to give it more of a vintage look. When everything is fully dry, add the heart to a leather lace. Overlap the lacing ends and secure with a barrel knot (see page 31).

Tip: Making a barrel knot over the overlapping ends creates an adjustable size necklace. Pull on the lacing ends to make the necklace smaller, or pull the sides of the loop to make it larger.

birds in flight earrings

Nature is a huge source of inspiration to me. These earrings are reminiscent of the long flowing tail feathers from exotic birds of paradise.

1 Punch out (see page 24) a small circle from the leather.

2 Punch out a larger circle around the small one so it sits off center.

1 Punch out (see page 24) a small circle from the leather.

YOU WILL NEED

* 1½ x 3 in. (4 x 7.5 cm) piece of white textured leather
* 2 flat leather lacing, each around 6 in. (15 cm) long
* 4 lengths of decorative cord, each around 8 in. (20 cm) long
* 2 lengths of decorative chain, each around 10 in. (20 cm) long
* Pair of fishhook earring wires
* 6 silver jump rings
* Circle punch in two sizes
* Hammer
* Poly block
* Scissors
* 2 pairs of pliers

3 Take one strip of flat leather lacing, a length of cord, and a length of chain and thread through the center of the circle. Hold everything together and secure with a barrel knot (see page 31) using another length of the cord. Trim the lengths of leather and cord to the desired length.

4 Attach two jump rings (see page 30) to the top of the leather circle and secure them together with an additional jump ring. Attach the earring wire as shown and close the loop. Repeat the steps to make a second earring.

Tip: In my earrings the large circle is around ³/₄ in. (2 cm) in diameter and the inner circle is around ³/₈ in. (1 cm). I always find it quicker to punch the smallest circle first. It is much easier to align the larger circle over the smaller one and position it where desired.

my favorite things bracelet

I like to collect charms from places I've traveled or those that represent my hobbies. That's why I call this "my favorite things."

YOU WILL NEED

* 6 in. (15 cm) leather band, 1 in. (2.5 cm) wide
* 3 in. (7.5 cm) leather strip, ¼ in. (5 mm) wide
* 2 brass eyelets
* 2 rhinestone rivets
* 4 large brass jump rings
* 2 small brass jump rings
* 2 small brass lobster clasps
* Rhinestone heart focal piece
* Miscellaneous charms
* Miscellaneous beads
* Spacer beads
* Decorative toggle clasp
* 2 headpins
* Rotary hole punch
* Hammer
* Rivet/eyelet setter
* Round-nose pliers

1 Use a rotary punch to cut a hole for the eyelet ¼ in. (6 mm) from each end. Set the eyelets (see page 25). Punch a second set of smaller holes for the rivets about 1½ in. (4 cm) further along at each end.

2 Cut the narrower strip of leather in half. Fold one piece over into a loop and punch a hole about ⅛ in. (3 mm) from the end. Insert a rivet through the hole in the loop and then through the bracelet band. Set in place using the rivet setter (see page 25). Repeat with the other loop on the other side. Thread a large jump ring (see page 30) onto each loop.

3 Create two dangles using the beads and headpins (see page 31). Attach a lobster clasp to each jump ring. Attach a small jump ring on each end of the heart charm and clip on the lobster clasps.

4 Attach the dangle and charms to the jump rings on the heart charm. Attach a large jump ring to each end through the eyelets. Attach a toggle clasp to the jump rings.

Tips: Measure your wrist and cut the leather band to fit exactly—when you add the clasp, this will give a little extra room for comfort.

When setting rhinestone rivets I place a piece of scrap leather into the rivet setter before adding the rhinestone. By doing this I cam protect the rhinestone from breaking when I hammer the rivet in place.

The rotary punch is a nice tool to have because you can easily switch between sizes when working on projects that use multiple size holes.

YOU WILL NEED

* About 7 in. (17.5 cm) of 18-gauge copper wire
* 37 in. (92.5 cm) of leather cord
* 20 in. (50 cm) of leather cord, cut in half
* Large bead
* Medium bead
* Round-nose pliers
* Hammer
* Bench block

This pretty and unusual necklace has no fastener—to wear it, place around the neck and drop the two beads through one of the loops of the spiral.

1 Using the pliers, bend one end of the wire into a spiral.

2 Continue bending to create a more zigzag effect above the spiral, and make a ring at the top. Hammer the shape flat, adding some texture with the hammer marks at the same time.

3 Fold the longer cord in half, yet slightly off center so one end is around 3 in. (7.5 cm) longer than the other. Insert the loop through the ring at the top of the copper spiral. Insert the cord ends through the cord loop. Pull tight and secure just above with a barrel knot (see page 31), using one of the 10 in. (25 cm) lengths of cord. Make a second barrel knot to hold the two strands together around 5 in. (12.5 cm) away.

Tip: If the wire doesn't bend easily, heat it up by holding it in a flame until it glows and then allow to cool. This is known as annealing and it will soften the wire so it will bend easily.

4 Thread the larger bead onto the longer cord end and knot above and below it to keep the bead in position. Trim off the end close to the final knot. Repeat to add the other bead to the other end.

key to my heart

When creating leather jewelry, you're bound to end up with small bits and pieces. I used these pieces to design this delicate necklace featuring an ordinary key as a pendant, decorated with a tiny leather flower.

1 Stamp a flower shape in a scrap of veg-tanned leather as described on page 26. Color the flower with a pink marker (see page 27). Color another area of the leather in green for leaves. Cut the flower out neatly with scissors.

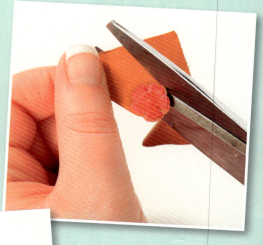

2 Snip between each petal of the flower, being careful only to cut to the edge of the center. Cut out a few leaves from the green area.

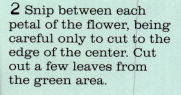

3 Fold the flower up into a cup shape and glue it to the head of the key. Add a few leaves around it. Add a bit of jewelry adhesive and attach seed beads to the centre of the flower.

Tips: You might find it easier to pick up the tiny flower and leaves using tweezers or the tips of a pair of pliers.

For added depth, use various hues of pinks and greens.

4 Thread the key onto the ribbon and lacing. Place a pair of ends together and add a crimp end. Close in place firmly with the pliers. Add the clasp to the ring of the crimp ends.

purple waterfall

* Purple flat leather lacing
* Pendant of your choice
* Cord end lobster clasp
* Clear silicone-based glue
* Toothpick

I took inspiration for this necklace from a colorful fountain just outside my hotel while on a recent trip to California—purple lights danced across the surface of the water as it came down the waterfall. Versatility is the highlight of this necklace because you can change the focal piece quite easily to match different outfits.

1 Measure and cut four the strands of lacing to the desired length. Gather the four ends together evenly and add a small dab of glue to secure.

2 Slide one of the metal cord ends on over the glue and allow to dry. Repeat the steps to add the other cord end onto the other end of the gathered lacing.

3 Slide the pendant onto the lacing to hang from the center.

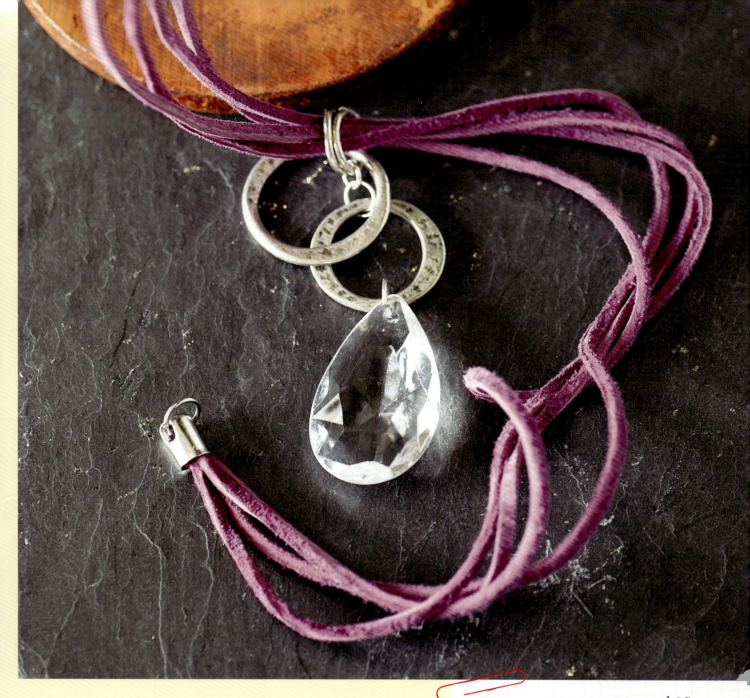

4 The lobster clasp attached to one cord end clips onto a ring attached to the other cord end, which makes this a quick and easy type of clasp.

Tip: This necklace has a small neat clasp and the focal pendant has a large jump ring so the pendant could be added after the clasp is in place. A big advantage of this is that you can substitute different pendants later without remaking the necklace. If you use a pendant with a smaller ring, you may need to add it to the lacing before adding the second cord end.

hello sunshine ring

Knock them out with this knuckleduster of a ring—which still manages to be ultra feminine with its pretty flower.

1 Use the template on page 120 to draw a spiral onto the reverse of the leather. Cut out the spiral.

2 Snip at about ⅛ in. (3 mm) intervals all along the outer edge of the spiral, stopping just before the inner edge. Leave the very center circle of the spiral uncut.

3 Starting from the outside, roll the spiral up tightly to make the flower, adding dabs of glue at intervals to keep the layers in place. Allow to dry.

4 The center circle forms a flat base to glue the flower securely in place onto the disk of the ring finding. Finish by adding the pearl bead into the center of the flower with a dab of glue.

Tip: For a little more glitz, add a small rhinestone flower in the center of the leather flower instead of the pearl bead.

loop de loop

Inspired by my favorite soup girls at a food market in London. What they make is delicious and colorful so I created three bracelets in one, all looped around each other; each one is simple to make and adding all the "ingredients" together creates a combination that is absolutely colorful and delicious! Add extra charms or beads as you prefer—bling it up baby!

1 Cut the brown flat lacing into three equal lengths and clip the ends together. Bring the right hand strand over into the center.

YOU WILL NEED

* Approx. 30 in. (75 cm) of dark brown flat leather lacing
* Approx. 30 in. (60 cm) of rust color boho braided lacing
* 12 in. (30 cm) of green flat leather lacing
* 1 large silver ring
* 24-gauge silver wire
* 6 in. (15 cm) of silver chain
* Large lobster clasp with cord ends
* 2 small lobster clasps with cord ends
* Large hole European-style butterfly bead
* Two pairs of pliers
* Clothespin or clip
* Glue

2 Next bring the left hand strand over into the center. Repeat these steps.

3 Continue until the braid is around 6 in. (15 cm) long, tightening the strands as you go for a neat and even braid. Glue each set of ends into a large cord end/lobster clasp assembly.

4 Wrap the boho braided lacing around your wrist at least three times, so when the ends meet it forms a comfortable but slightly snug bracelet.

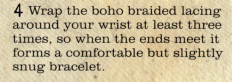

5 Glue each end of the braid lacing into the cord ends on either side of one of the small lobster clasps.

6 Thread the butterfly bead onto the cord. Make sure you are using a large hole bead so that you can interchange or add additional beads later.

7 Cut the green lacing in half. Fold one length over the silver ring and bring the ends together. Bind with a little silver wire next to the silver ring to hold the loop in place. Repeat on the other side of the ring.

8 Cut the chain in half. Open an end link in the same way as you would a jump ring (see page 30) and clip it onto the silver ring. Repeat on the other side of the ring.

9 Glue each pair of lacing ends into the cord end on either side of one of the small lobster clasps. Use jump rings to attach each chain end to the ring on opposite sides of the lobster clasp. Wear all three bracelets on the same wrist.

butterfly
key cover

When it's night time and all my keys look alike, it's hard to find just which one I want to use. I solved this dilemma by using different colors of leather and charms, and now they're decorative too!

Tip: Key heads can be different sizes so before you begin check the template is big enough to enclose the key with extra on each side to allow space for the stitching. Bigger is better, you can always trim the excess away after stitching.

YOU WILL NEED

* 2¾ x 1¾ in. (7 x 4.5 cm) piece of leather
* 2 eyelets
* Split ring
* Jump ring
* Swivel lobster clasp
* Butterfly charm
* Brown waxed stitching thread
* Poly block
* Bench block
* Hammer
* ⅛ in. (3 mm) 4-prong lacing chisel
* Stitching awl
* Punch
* Eyelet setter
* Leather scissors
* 2 pairs of pliers

1 Cut the leather using the template on page 120. Fold over the head of the key and mark the position of the hole at the top. Remove the key and punch (see page 24) the appropriate sized hole to match the eyelet size through both layers of the leather.

2 Open out the leather and set an eyelet in each hole, as described on page 25.

3 Fold the leather over and stitch down each side in turn, using saddlestitch (see page 28).

4 Insert the key again and add the split ring through the eyelets and through the hole in the key. Add the swivel lobster clasp and the butterfly charm to the split ring using a jump ring (see page 30).

butterfly key cover

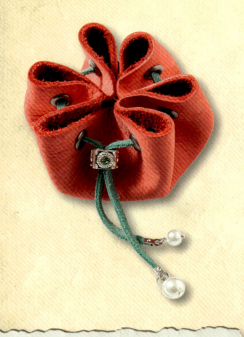

jewelry gift pouch

Ideal to use when giving a gift of jewelry, this simple but stunning pouch is also great for carrying your valuables when traveling.

1 Cut a circle measuring 5¼ in. (13.5 cm) in diameter from the leather. Punch 12 holes (see page 24) spaced evenly and positioned about ¼ in. (1 cm) in from the edge. Add an eyelet in each hole and set (see page 25). Thread the lacing in and out all around, bringing both lacing ends through to the outside in the last pair of holes.

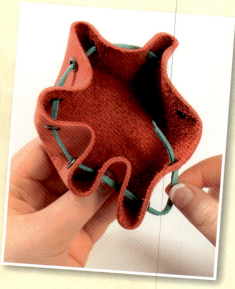

YOU WILL NEED

* 6 in. (15 cm) square of coral leather
* 10 in. (25 cm) of aqua leather lacing
* 12 eyelets
* European bead
* 2 pearl beads
* 2 headpins
* Jump ring
* 2 cord ends
* Punch
* Bench block
* Poly block
* Hammer
* Eyelet setter
* 2 pairs of pliers

2 Add a cord end at each end of the lacing and crimp in place. Bring the two ends of the lacing together and thread on the bead and the jump ring.

3 Make two pearl dangles following the instructions on page 31. Add a dangle onto each cord end.

Tip: The jump ring should be slightly tighter on the cords than the bead; it keeps the bead in place when the cord is pulled to close the pouch.

daisy may

Make sure those pesky glasses never get lost again with this eye-popping psychedelic daisy-patterned case. Or make up your own design if you are feeling artistic.

1 Fold the leather in half and place the straight edge of the template on page 123 against the fold line. Cut out and then punch holes (see page 24) all around the cut edge. Whipstitch (see page 30) around each curved edge separately. At the end of the curved section, begin whipstitching through both layers together to join the bottom and sides.

2 Paint two circles in magenta around 1½ in. (4 cm) in diameter for the center of the flowers, using the photograph as a guide for positioning. Let dry. Add a slightly smaller circle of orange on top of this, then a circle of yellow, and finally a small circle of magenta for the very center of the flower.

3 Add big petals in white, radiating out from the edge of the center circles. Leave to dry. Add slightly smaller blue petals on top of the white.

Tip: Don't fuss about the painting—you only need a few basic skills and your flowers will look great. This project really comes together when the doodles and extra detail are added. I left mine just painted, but you might want to add your own bling!

4 Add details—I put lots of dots of different colors in the center of my flowers, outlined the petals and dots roughly in gel pen, then added some highlighting in white and extra small flowers between the larger ones. Copy my design or just make up your own!

chapter 2

make it masculine

rivet cuff

The glint of silver eyelets adds a touch of steampunk charm to this simple leather cuff. You can add more decoration if you choose, but sometimes simplicity is best!

YOU WILL NEED

* Ready-made veg-tanned leather cuff with snaps
* 5 eyelets
* Leather dye
* Cosmetic sponge
* Poly block
* Rotary hole punch
* Hammer
* Bench block
* Rivet/eyelet setter

1 Apply leather dye to the cosmetic sponge and wipe it onto the front of cuff to give it a more vintage look.

2 Measure and mark five holes spaced evenly around the cuff. Punch the holes.

Tip: To give the cuff a more feminine look, you could thread pretty ribbon or a delicate silver chain in and out through the holes.

3 Insert an eyelet through one of the holes from the front to the back of the cuff. Place the eyelet right side down onto a poly block. Insert the setter and give a firm tap with the hammer to set the eyelet. Repeat in the other holes.

rivet cuff

interlaced chain

Super-simple yet a great look! This chain and leather combo is one of my easy projects that anyone can tackle with confidence.

make it masculine

YOU WILL NEED

* ¾ x 7 in. (2 x 18 cm) of green-gray leather
* Brown leather cord
* 6½ in. (17 cm) of brass chain
* 2 brass jump rings
* 2 spring beads
* Brass lobster clasp
* Hole punch
* Poly block
* Hammer

1 Punch holes along each side of the leather strip about ¼ in. (6 mm) apart. Fold the leather cord in half and thread the ends into the two holes on the end, bringing the cords up on the wrong side of the leather.

2 Place the chain along the leather. Insert the leather cord ends through the first link of chain. Bring the right end over the leather strip, through the hole and then up through the next chain link. Repeat for the left side. Continue to the end.

3 Knot the cord ends together, trim off the ends, and hide the knot inside the chain. Add a jump ring through the last two holes at each end (see page 30). Attach a spring bead to each jump ring and the lobster clasp to the spring beads.

Tip: Odd short lengths of chain can be hard to use up, but this project is ideal to put them to good use. You can use a dab of glue to secure the knotted ends and prevent them from coming loose.

* ¾ x 20 in. (2 x 50 cm) strip of leather
* 3 x 5½ in. (7.5 x 14 cm) rectangle of leather
* ⅜ x 3 in. (1 x 7.5 cm) strip of leather
* 2 silver buckles
* Sewing awl
* Brown waxed stitching thread
* 4-prong chisel punch
* 1/16 in. (1.5 mm) hole punch
* Poly block
* Hammer
* Leather scissors
* Sewing needle

buckled up

Nothing feminine about this bold statement cuff for the guy in your life! To spice it up even more, consider adding a few pointed studs for a very rugged and masculine look.

1 Cut the 20-in. (50-cm) strip of leather in half. Measure down by about 1 in. (2.5 cm) from the end and punch a hole for the buckle prong. Thread the buckle prong through the hole. Repeat for the second strap.

2 Fold the end of the strip over and punch stitching holes (see page 28). Saddlestitch across to hold the buckle in place. Repeat for the other strap. Cut the opposite end of the strap into a blunt-tipped triangle. Punch holes in each strap as marked on the template on page 120.

3 Trim the rectangle of leather to fit the base template on page 120 and round off the corners. Lay the first strap down on the base, as marked on the template, with the buckle flush against one short edge. Saddlestitch the strap and cuff together along one edge for 2 in. (5 cm) below the buckle and finish off with a knot. Fold the cuff away and saddlestitch only the strap all the way around and back to the last 2 in. (5 cm). Finish with a knot. Fold the cuff back and stitch the strap and cuff together up to the buckle. Finish and knot. Repeat for the other strap.

4 Place the 3-in. (7.5-cm) strip of leather over all layers near the buckle. Punch a set of 4 holes through the strip and cuff for the cross stitches. Using the needle, make a cross stitch through all layers to secure the straps.

* 48 in. (120 cm) of beige leather lacing
* 3 lengths of leather lacing, each 6 in. (15 cm)
* Brown waxed stitching thread
* Stone arrowhead
* Scissors

Any guy would be pleased with this authentic stone arrowhead necklace, which is much easier to make than it might look.

1 Cut the long piece of lacing in half. Fold one length in half and make a barrel knot (see page 31) using the brown thread just above the center point, to create a small loop of lacing.

2 Open out the two ends of the lacing in a deep V with the loop at the bottom. Lay the second length of lacing above in a shallower U-shape. Make a barrel knot on each side to hold the two cords together, this time using two of the 6 in. (15 cm) lengths of leather lacing.

3 Fold over one longer end to make a loop and make a barrel knot over both strands using the third short length of leather lacing. Trim any long ends.

4 At the other end, knot both ends together to make a round knot that will fit through the loop to act as a toggle. Trim any long ends.

5 Cut a 10 in. (25 cm) length of brown waxed stitching thread. Loop it in half behind the arrowhead, bring the ends into the grooves on each side and cross them over at the front.

6 Turn the arrowhead over and cross the ends over again at the back.

7 Wrap the left end right around the top groove from left to right, and the right end around to the left.

make it masculine

8 Tie the threads ends together in a half-knot.

9 Take both thread ends through the loop at the bottom of the necklace.

Tip: After you tie the half-knot, it will pull up to the top of the arrowhead, but this will not matter if the previous wraps are good and tight.

10 Make a barrel knot using the two thread ends to hold the arrowhead in place. Pull tight and then trim off the ends close to the knot.

arrowhead necklace

- Old baseball glove
- Watch face
- 7 rivets
- Buckle
- Metal rule
- Utility knife
- Hole punch
- Poly block
- Hammer
- Rivet setting tool

baseball mitt watchstrap

An excellent way to upcycle old leather sports items, this watchstrap makes use of the logos or text that is already printed on the leather. If someone is a particular fan, you may be able to find something that features their favorite team or the signature of a sports personality.

1 Decide which area of the mitt you want to feature and cut out two straps, one 4¾ in. (12 cm) and the other 5½ in. (14 cm) long. Both straps should be about ¾ in. (2 cm) wide or to fit the lugs on the side of the watch. Cut one end of the shorter strap into a blunt point and punch a few holes at about ¾ in. (2 cm) intervals.

2 Cut a narrow 3¼-in. (8-cm) long strip of leather and rivet into a loop (see page 25). Attach the strap to the watch by folding the square end of the watchstrap through the watch lug on the bottom and back down by about ¾ in. (2 cm). Rivet in place. Repeat for the longer strap on the other side of the watch.

3 Thread the loop onto the longer strap, rivet side down. Punch a hole for the buckle prong about 1 in. (2.5 cm) from the end of the longer strap. Thread the buckle prong through the hole, bend the end over, and rivet in place.

Tip: If you cannot find a length long enough on the glove for the strap, try sewing multiple pieces together with a saddlestitch to make up the length. You can also mix and match leathers in the strap—but make sure that different leathers look as if they are part of the design and not a mistake from having too little leather.

leather 'n' studs

YOU WILL NEED

* Strip of black leather about 1¼ in. (3 cm) wide
* Approx. 24 in. (60 cm) of boho braided lacing
* Black waxed stitching thread
* Stainless steel screw U-knob
* 2 flat-head nickel finish rivets
* 3 button stud brads
* Punch
* Poly block
* Hammer
* Rivet setter
* 2-hole punch
* Oval punch
* Glue

This look is great for guys and gals! For the guys add a bulkier clasp, or for a little biker chic exchange the clasp for something a little lighter in weight. Studded, riveted, and knotted—my kind of project!

1 Fold over each end of the leather strip by approximately 1 in. (2.5 cm) and punch a hole for the rivet. Set the rivets as explained on page 25. Using the 2-hole punch, punch three pairs of holes for the button stud brads, evenly spaced around the bracelet. Set the button stud brads as explained on page 77.

2 Punch two oval holes 1 in. (2.5 cm) apart between rivet and button stud brad and between each pair of button studs brads. Thread the lacing through the folded end above the rivet and bring the two ends down behind the bracelet. Thread the two ends through the first oval hole up to the front.

Tip: Measure your wrist and add at least 3 in. (7.5 cm) to allow for the folded ends and to make sure the bracelet is not too tight. Cut the strip of leather to this length. You can make the bracelet shorter to fit when you fold over the ends if you need to.

3 Take the lacing down through the next hole to the back. Continue around the bracelet, bringing the ends alternately to the front and the back. At the other end, take the right end through the folded end above the rivet from right to left. Take the left end through from left to right.

4 Bring both braided lacing ends down together and secure them just below the rivet using a barrel knot (see page 31). Use a dab of glue to hold the ends under the flap below the rivet. Add one half of the clasp to the loop at each end.

lone star keychain

This chunky star-studded keychain is the ideal gift for the man in your life—ideal to store those important keys.

YOU WILL NEED

* 7 x 1¼ in. (12.5 x 3 cm) strip of leather
* Approximately 14 small silver brads
* Star screw post
* D-ring
* Brown waxed thread
* Swivel lobster clasp
* Poly block
* Hammer
* 4-prong lacing chisel
* Stitching awl
* Leather scissors
* Punch
* Pair of pliers
* Screwdriver

1 Fold over one end of the leather by ¾ in. (2 cm) and cut off each corner on the diagonal so the folded edge fits the width of the bar on swivel lobster clasp.

2 Slide the lobster clasp onto the end. Fold the leather over again and then saddlestitch across (see page 28). Attach the D-ring to the other end in the same way, although there is no need to make the diagonal cuts.

3 Using an appropriate size punch, make a line of evenly spaced pairs of holes through the upper layer of leather only, just below the stitching at the D-ring end—you need two holes for each brad, one for each prong. Insert the brad prongs through the holes.

4 On the reverse, fold the flap of leather back out of the way and use a pair of pliers to turn the prongs of the brads outward to secure them. Add a row of brads at the other end in the same way.

Tip: You can use any screw post decoration on this—or make up your own decoration using a technique from one of the other projects.

5 Punch a hole for the star focal pendant as explained on page 24. Push the post of the star through the hole and secure with the accompanying screw.

man's choker

The bold, chunky feel and the earth-tone color of this choker lend a rugged masculine touch. It's a simple and quick project to make as a gift for the special guy in your life!

1 Apply a small amount of glue to the wrong side of the leather strip and fold both long edges inward to meet at the center. Allow to dry completely.

2 Add a length of black boho braided lacing to cover the joint.

3 Secure the lacing in place with barrel knots (see page 31) using the black waxed cord at approximately 2½ in. (6.5 cm) intervals along the length of the choker.

4 Glue one half of a magnetic cord end clasp at each end of the choker.

* 15 in. (45 cm) square of veg-tanned leather
* 8 in. (20 cm) of brown leather lacing
* Dark brown stamping inkpad
* Bicycle stamp
* Brown waxed stitching thread
* Tan leather dye
* Utility knife
* Half-circle punch
* Poly block
* Hammer
* ⅛ in. (3 mm) 4-prong lacing chisel
* Stitching awl
* Cosmetic sponge
* Cutting mat

let's go places tag

Travel in style with this smart leather luggage tag, which you can add to any suitcase or overnight bag. You can use any stamp on it, to personalize to your own taste.

1 Using the template on page 124, cut out two of the tag shape from veg-tanned leather. Cut around the edges of the flap shape on one tag piece only.

2 Using the half-circle punch, cut out a half-moon shape from the piece with the flap cut. Place the two pieces together and punch stitching holes all the way around. Saddlestitch (see page 28) the bottom edge individually on each tag. Place the tags together and saddlestitch around the sides and top. Punch a hole through all layers just below the stitching at the center of the shaped end.

3 Apply ink to the bicycle stamp and press onto the front of the tag, using the photograph as a guide for position. Allow to dry.

4 Sponge a little dye over both sides of the tag. Allow to dry completely.

5 Fold the lacing in half. Feed the loop through the hole in the tag and then feed the lacing ends through the loop. Tie the ends together in a knot.

mystical braid

* 2 x 16 in. (5 x 40 cm) of leather
* 2 screw-in button studs
* Pen
* Metal rule
* Cutting mat
* Utility knife
* Hole punch
* Poly block
* Hammer

Once you get the hang of the braiding technique, this bracelet is really easy to make—but it looks as if you have magically rejoined the leather strips after braiding them! I like the simplicity of this as it is, but you could add extra studs or rivets to decorate the edges of the plain section if you choose.

1 Using the template on page 123, cut out the main shape from the leather. Copy the cutting lines onto the leather. Using a utility knife and metal rule, cut the two long slits for the braided section and the slot for the end to thread through.

2 Lay the piece out vertically, right side up. Bring the end of the slotted section up through the hole between the center and the right strand. Pull it down so that the bottom of the strap is on the right side.

3 The leather strips may look a bit tangled now, as shown here. However, it's important not to omit the next step.

4 At the top, braid the left strand over the center strand toward the right and the right strand over the center strand toward the left. Finally take the left strand over the center strand again toward the right to create a neat flat braid with the right side facing you as shown. Think left-right-left. Don't worry about the twists going on at the bottom.

5 Create an opening between the left and center loop and bring the end up through this opening and then down. It is similar to step 2 except this time we are working on the left side.

Tip: The template given will make a finished bracelet around 6½–7 in. (16.5–18 cm) in circumference. If you need a bigger bracelet, lengthen by the extra amount needed at two points: between the slot and the start of the braided section and by the same amount within the braided section.

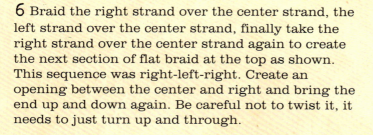

6 Braid the right strand over the center strand, the left strand over the center strand, finally take the right strand over the center strand again to create the next section of flat braid at the top as shown. This sequence was right-left-right. Create an opening between the center and right and bring the end up and down again. Be careful not to twist it, it needs to just turn up and through.

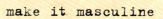

7 Braid the left strand over the center strand toward the right, take the right strand over the center strand toward the left, finally take the left strand over the center strand again toward the right. This sequence is left-right-left. Create an opening between the left and center. Bring the end up and through the opening.

8 The completed braid may look a bit messy but don't worry. Work along with your fingers making sure that each strip is facing up and that all the braiding is even.

9 Set the two screw-in button studs (see step 5 on page 77) as marked on the template at the plain end. Punch two holes at the braided end. Thread the end of the braid up through the slot in the bracelet and around.

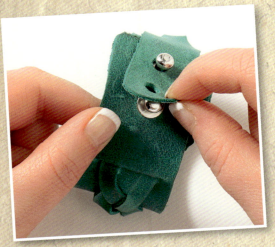

10 Press the button studs through the holes to secure the bracelet; having two studs makes the bracelet adjustable.

chapter 3

mix and re-make it

book of quotes

Make your own miniature book of quotes by writing inspirational words on the pages of this tiny book, which you can then wear around your neck. Or consider writing a personal note inside and give it to someone special as a gift.

1 Emboss the leather (see page 26) or use textured leather. Cut a rectangle 1½ x 3 in. (4 x 7.5 cm) and fold in half, making the book cover. Punch a small hole near the top in the center of the spine and another on the back at the bottom right corner.

(see page 26)

2 Fold a piece of paper in half three times so you have eight layers. With the single folded edge as the spine, cut the pages to 1½ in. (4 cm) high by 1¼ in. (3 cm) wide. Add a dab of glue along the spine of each page layer and stack together. Glue inside the cover.

3 Place the finding on the front of the book from top to bottom and fold the ends over to the inside. Punch a hole on the front right center of the book cover and set a small eyelet (see page 25). Repeat for the back cover. Thread the string through the eyelet holes and tie in a bow. Add a jump ring to the hole in the spine and then add a second jump ring in that. Add a jump ring to the hole in the back bottom right corner.

(see page 25)

YOU WILL NEED

* 4 in. (10 cm) square of leather
* Embossing folder
* Long decorative brass finding
* 2 small eyelets
* Short length of string
* 4 brass jump rings
* Headpin
* Crystal bead
* Brass bead cap
* Brass spacer bead
* Small brass charm
* Brass key charm
* 25 in. (62.5 cm) of ball chain with fastener
* 4 x 5 in. (10 x 12.5 cm) piece of paper
* Pasta or embossing machine
* Leather scissors
* Eyelet setter
* Hole punch
* Poly block
* Hammer
* Scissors
* Clear silicone-based glue
* Pliers

Tip: I chose a finding for my book that had a frame in which to write a word. I also added a bit of color to it with alcohol ink to highlight the details.

4 Make up a dangle with the headpin and beads as described on page 31. Add the dangle and the small charm to the second jump ring at the top of the book. Add the key charm to the jump ring at the bottom. Use another jump ring to attach the book to the length of ball chain.

* Baseball
* Decorative finding with a screw post
* Filigree pendant back
* Lobster clasp
* 2 jump rings
* Orange thread
* Utility knife
* Sewing needle
* Alcohol-based marker
* Hole punch
* Hammer
* Poly block
* Screwdriver
* 2 pairs of pliers

baseball cuff

What could be a better gift for a sports fan than this neat cuff made from part of a baseball? Add any embellishment that you choose for a range of different looks.

1 Carefully slice through the stitching to remove the shaped leather covering pieces from the baseball.

2 Using orange thread, whipstitch (see page 30) along the edges using the original holes. Secure the thread end with a knot.

3 If needed, color the finding to match your project. Here I used an alcohol-based marker. Punch a hole in the center front of the cuff, push the post of the finding through, and screw in the back. Glue the filigree pendant to the finding and let dry.

4 Add a lobster clasp to the back of the cuff using jump rings through a pair of the stitching holes.

turquoise sunset earrings

These pretty earrings were inspired by a colorful
sunset after a recent storm; mix and match colors
to suit your mood or to match a favorite outfit.

YOU WILL NEED

* Scraps of leather in coral, pale pink, and turquoise
* 10 tiny silver jump rings
* 2 pairs of pliers
* 2 ribbon ends
* 2 earring wires
* Leather scissors
* Hole punch
* Poly block
* Hammer

1 Using the templates on page 121, cut out two bottom shapes in coral, two middle shapes in pale pink, and two top shapes in turquoise. Punch three holes (see page 24) along the top edge of each bottom piece and three matching holes along the bottom edge of each middle piece. Cut slits along bottom edge of each bottom piece to create a fringe.

2 Punch two holes along the top edge of each middle piece and two matching holes along the bottom edge of each top piece. Join each set of three pieces together in order with tiny jump rings (see page 30).

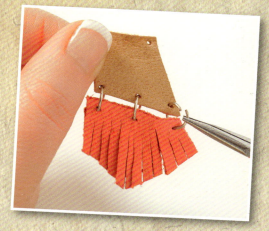

3 Add a ribbon end to the top of each top piece. Add an earring wire to the ring of each ribbon end.

Tip: These earrings only use a small amount of leather, so they are ideal to use up those odd scraps left over from other projects. I hate to throw bits away! If you don't have these colors, play with other combinations to create your own unique pair.

YOU WILL NEED

* 2 x 4 in. (5 x 10 cm) of veg-tanned leather
* Acrylic paint in green, turquoise, blue-green, red, and brown
* 4 turquoise chips
* 4 headpins
* 8 jump rings
* 2 round spacers
* 2 earring wires
* 15 in. (45 cm) of chain
* Leather scissors
* Paintbrush
* Hole punch
* Poly block
* Hammer
* 2 pairs of pliers

feather dangles

Bring out your inner Pocahontas with these dangling feather and turquoise earrings, which look as if they came straight from an expensive boho chic store.

1 Use the templates on page 123 to cut two of each size feather, one of each for each earring. Paint the smaller feathers in green tipped with turquoise and then deep blue-green (see page 27 for painting instructions). Paint the larger feathers in red tipped with brown. Let dry, then cut slits into each feather along both side edges to create more of a feathered effect. Punch a small hole in the top of each.

2 Make up a dangle (see page 31) by adding a turquoise chip to a headpin, creating a loop at the top and inserting the end of a ½ in. (7.5 mm) length of chain. Repeat using a 1 in. (2.5 cm) length of chain. Cut two 1½ in. (4 cm) lengths of chain and two 4 in. (10 cm) lengths. Add a long and short dangle to a jump ring. Add a long and short chain to another jump ring. Create a second set of dangles and chains for the second earring.

3 Stack a small feather on top of a large one and add a jump ring through the holes. Before closing the jump ring, add the long and short dangle on the front and the long and short chain on the back. Close the jump ring. Repeat with the second earring.

4 Add a little turquoise paint to each circular spacer bead and on the ball of each earring wire. Use another jump ring to add the circular spacer to the top of the earring assembly. On the other side of the circular spacer add the earring wire. Repeat for the second earring.

YOU WILL NEED

* * 4 in. (10 cm) square of pink leather
* * 4 in. (10 cm) square of beige leather
* * Approx. 22 in. (55 cm) of boho braided lacing
* * 2 rhinestone flowers
* * 4 small rhinestones
* * Crystal bead
* * Alcohol-based felt-tip markers in deep pink, blue, and two shades of green
* * 2 pearl beads
* * Headpin
* * Scrap of fine chain
* * Clear silicone-based glue
* * Crimp cord ends
* * Clasp of your choice
* * Leather scissors
* * Pair of pliers

Delicate flowers combined with pearls and sparkling rhinestones create a romantic and delicate necklace. Changing the color of the flowers could give this necklace a completely new look—try white for apple blossom, red or pink for roses, or yellow for gerbera.

1 Using the flower template on page 121, cut four flowers from the pink leather. Trim two of the flowers down so they are slightly smaller. Stack the flowers on top of each other, color the petal edges slightly with the marker (see page 27), and curve into shape with your fingers. Stick a rhinestone flower in the center of each.

2 Cut three tiny squares from the beige leather. Shape into flowers and color blue with a marker. Add a single rhinestone in the center of each. Use the leaf template to cut four leaves from the beige leather. Fringe the leaf edges and color with the green markers. Lay the braided lacing out flat and arrange the flowers and leaves attractively on top.

3 When you are happy the arrangement, glue in place. Glue a scrap of leather onto the back for added stability. Add in additional beads. Make up a dangle (see page 31) and attach to the bottom of the chain. Glue one end of the chain beneath a flower so the dangle hangs free. Attach the crimp cord ends and a clasp of your choice.

Tip: I like to use alcohol-based markers because they blend nicely and give a graduated shading effect.

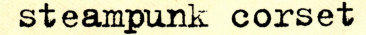

steampunk corset

The essence of vintage style, this chunky bracelet combines leather, lace, and metal cogwheels with Victorian lacing in delicate silky ribbons at the back.

1 Trace the spiral template on page 120 onto the wrong side of the pink leather and then cut out. Repeat to cut a spiral for the second flower.

2 Begin at the angled edged and roll up a spiral to form the rose. Allow the spiral to open slightly. Secure with glue onto the round base at the center.

3 Using your fingers, shape the petals outward to form the flower. Make the second flower in the same way.

4 Sponge a little antiquing stain over the petals to give them an authentic vintage look.

5 Punch stitching holes (see page 28) into the brown leather and turn over so that the wrong side is facing up. Add the lace right side down in the center as shown. Fold over the two leather ends and stitch across the top and bottom edges using saddlestitch.

Tip: The folded-over leather flaps on the inside of the cuff are open at the ends inside, forming little secret pockets to store small items.

6 Arrange the lace motif on the front of the cuff in a pleasing design and stick into place with glue.

7 Position the roses attractively on top of the lace motif, roughly in the center, and secure with glue.

8 Collage pearls, watch parts, and other elements to create a pleasing design, then glue to secure.

9 Set three eyelets (see page 25) at each end of the cuff. Lace the ribbon through the eyelets and pull up like a corset.

steampunk corset

diamond drop earrings

These earrings are super easy to make but
look stunning. They are also ideal for using
up those small scraps of pretty leather that
you just can't bear to throw away.

YOU WILL NEED

* Scrap of textured leather
* 4 silver rhinestone charms
* 2 diamond-shape charms
* 2 earring wires
* 4 silver jump rings
* Pen or pencil
* Leather scissors
* Punch
* Poly block
* Hammer
* 2 pairs of pliers

1 Copy the template on page 124 onto the reverse of the leather twice and cut out two pieces.

2 Fold up the points of one piece to meet at the top and punch a small hole just below the tip (see page 24). Add a jump ring (see page 30). Before closing the jump ring, add a rhinestone charm on one side of the leather loop, the diamond-shape charm in the middle, and the other charm on the back. Close the jump ring.

3 Add the earring wire to the top of the diamond shape charm with another jump ring. Repeat steps 2–3 for the other earring.

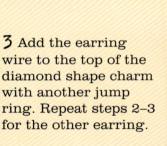

Tips: You need to hang a charm on the front and the back of the loop of leather to counterbalance, otherwise the earring will not hang straight.

If you don't have textured leather, you can create your own using the technique on page 26.

* Purchased embossed leather belt
* 8¾ in. (22.5 cm) of lace trim
* 2 button studs
* Screw post set
* Butterfly finding
* Acrylic paint in purple and black
* Hole punch
* Poly block
* Hammer
* Paintbrush
* Cosmetic sponge
* Clear silicone-based glue
* Screwdriver

flower power

Plain embossed belt lengths are ideal for re-purposing into something much more interesting. Add color, lace, and a decorative finding for a bracelet with a completely new look.

1 Measure your wrist and add 3 in. (7.5 cm)—I cut a piece of belt 8¾ in. (22.5 cm) long. Paint the belt with purple acrylic paint and allow to dry. Wipe black acrylic over the top.

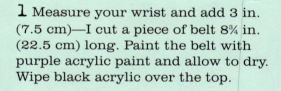

2 Wipe the black away while it is still wet, leaving enough just to highlight the embossed design on the belt. Glue the length of lace down the center of the bracelet. Punch out two holes for the studs ¼ in. (5 mm) from one end and a second pair ¾ in. (2 cm) from the other end for fastening.

Tip: To make the bracelet adjustable, add extra pairs of studs so you can choose which set to fasten on.

Using a screw post focal piece allows you to change the center piece to match your outfit.

3 Screw in the button studs. Punch a hole (see page 24) in the center of the bracelet for the screw-post butterfly. If you can't find something you like, you can make your own screw-post finding by gluing the post of the screw post set to the back of any finding. Allow it to dry before attaching.

4 Push the post through the center hole and screw on the back.

bling your boots!

Designer boots cost a fortune: save your money and customize a plain pair of boots to look twice as good by making a pair of these studded boot bands.

* 1¼ x 15 in. (3 x 37.5 cm) strip of brown leather —adjust length as needed
* 26 square stud brads
* 24 round stud brads
* 2 latch-hook fastenings
* 2-prong brad punch
* Pair of pliers
* 4 rivets
* Poly block
* Ruler
* Hammer
* Rivet setting block

1 Measure along both edges of the band to space out the brads around ½ in. (12 mm) apart. Punch a pair of holes (see page 24) for each brad in the marked positions.

2 Push the prongs of the brad through the pair of holes. On the reverse, bend the prongs down with pliers to lay flat.

3 Place the parts of the fastening on the boot ends and mark the position of all the holes. Punch the holes and attach the fastener in place with rivets (see page 25).

Tips: My fashion tip— buy plain, classic style boots and make lots of boot bands to coordinate with different outfits. Mix and match and layer them together for a very trendy look!

Some of the other projects in this book could also be adapted as boot bands; try the Rivet Cuff (page 62), Leather 'n' Studs (page 74), or Man's Choker (page 78).

* Old black leather boot
* 8 x 15 in. (20 x 37.5 cm) of black leather
* 3 pointed screw studs
* Acrylic paint in yellow, orange, and red
* Black waxed stitching thread
* Utility knife
* Metal rule
* Paintbrush
* Leather scissors
* Half-circle punch
* Poly block
* Hammer
* Hole punch
* Screwdriver
* Awl needle
* Sewing needle

up in flames

Upcycle an old boot into a funky cellphone case designed to be threaded onto a belt for handsfree on the move. You don't even need a pair of boots—just one odd one will be enough for a couple of cases! I used the motif from my boot, but look for other decorative bits you can reuse.

1 Remove the leather from the boot with a utility knife. Choose a section of leather measuring about 2¾ in. (7 cm) wide and 7½ in. (19 cm) long and use the template on page 122 to cut the flap, using a pair of leather scissors or the utility knife.

2 To create the flame pattern, paint the design (see page 27) beginning with the yellow. You may have to give it a second coat to make the paint color stand out.

3 Paint the center portion of the flame with orange.

4 Finally, add red to the tips of the flame. Blend all colors together so that the color goes from yellow to orange to red.

5 Using the templates on page 122, cut the front and back pieces from matching black leather. Cut out a half circle in the center of the top edge of the front piece. Punch the holes (see page 24) and screw in the three studs in the positions marked on the template.

Tips: If you are not using a motif cut from a boot, you can still paint a design of your choice onto a piece of ordinary leather.

The measurements given here will make a case that fits an iPhone or similar. If you have a different model, check the size of your phone before cutting pieces.

6 On the back piece, measure 2½ in. (6.5 cm) down from the top. Overlap the top edge of the flap to this point. Create stitching holes and sew the flap to the back using whipstitch (see page 30). Cut a strip of leather ¾ in. (2 cm) and 15 in. (37.5 cm) long for the side piece. Punch stitching holes along both long edges. Sew one side of the strip around the sides and bottom of the front piece (see page 28 for sewing instructions).

7 Sew the sides and bottom of the back onto the other edge of the side strip, but don't sew through the flap. Fold the flap over to the front and mark the positions of the holes for the studs. Punch the three holes.

8 Using the needle, sew running stitch across the flap to attach it just below the top edge of the back— this creates the channel for a belt to slide through.

9 Whipstitch (see page 30) around the flap to finish the cut edges.

lil'birdy told me

This fun and whimsical pouch was designed to fit a larger mobile phone. The classic shape is a great base to show off your own individual style by changing the design on the front.

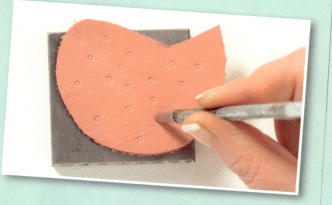

1 Use the templates on page 121 to cut a bird body from the pink leather. Cut the wing from yellow leather. Cut the front and the back of the case from off-white leather. Texture the bird body (see page 26) by stamping a design.

2 Saddlestitch (see page 28) the bird and wing to the front of the case. Also stitch an eye, a beak, and two legs. Place the back and front wrong sides together and blanket stitch (see page 30) around the edges to join.

YOU WILL NEED

* 8 in. (20 cm) square of off-white leather
* 2¾ in. (7 cm) square of pink leather
* Scrap of yellow leather
* Brown button
* Brown waxed stitching thread
* Clear silicone-based glue
* Snap fastener
* Leather design stamp
* Snap setter
* Leather scissors
* Hammer
* Bench block
* Needle

3 Set the snap. Sew a button over the snap position on the outside of the flap.

mix and re-make it

Tips: Since the snap is near the top of the pouch, you can set it after the pouch is made to get the positioning accurate.

Instead of sewing on a button to cover the snap, simply use a decorative snap instead.

Play with the size and position of the bird or desired motif to achieve a whole new look.

flip flap

This handy little bag takes a fair bit of work, but the techniques are all really simple so there is nothing to get stressed about. I used eyelets to attach the two sides because the posts on the rivets I had planned to use were too long, but I really like the retro look they have given the bag.

1 Cut a 25 x 7 in. (62.5 x 17.5 cm) piece of leather. I used the shaped edge that was already on the end of my length of leather as the flap, but you can cut it into any similar shape. Measure 8 in. (20 cm) from the bottom and 1½ in. (4 cm) from the side and mark two ¼ in. (6 mm) lines approximately ⅝ in. (1.5 cm) apart. Mark another set about ½ in. (12 mm) above this set. Cut the four slits.

2 From the remaining leather cut two pieces each 1¼ in. (3.5 cm) wide (or to fit the D-ring) and 3 in. (7.5 cm) long for the D-ring tabs. Fold a tab over the bar of the D-ring and on the back align the two ends together at the halfway mark. Punch four holes for the eyelets (see page 24). Repeat on the other tab.

3 Fold the straight edge of the bag over to the wrong side by ½ in. (12 mm) and glue in place to finish. Fold the bottom of the bag up by 9 in. (22.5 cm) with right sides out. Flip the bag over. Align the D-ring tabs with the folded edge underneath, so that they sit just over the top of the edge. Mark the four eyelet holes.

4 Mark further eyelet holes down at ½ in. (12 mm) intervals, right to the bottom of the bag on each side. Punch the two inner holes on the D-ring tab only through the tab and the bag back—don't punch them through the bag front. Punch all the remaining holes through all layers. Set an eyelet (see page 25) in each hole, joining the front and back together.

Tips: If you punch a hole in the wrong place—as I did when making the bag—you might be able to fix the situation by sticking a small square of the same leather on the back and gluing the punched holes back in.

Adjust the dimensions to fit a tablet. You can even make a pouch on the back side to fit your phone using the dimensions for the Lil' Birdy Told Me project on page 112.

Adding the leather strap to the center of the chain makes it a little more comfortable to carry, but if you prefer you can just use a longer length of chain and omit the strap section.

5 Divide the chain in half. Open the last chain link and slip onto the D-ring. Close the chain with pliers. Repeat on the other side. From the remaining leather cut a piece 1 in. (2.5 cm) by 10 in. (25 cm). Fold the ends over the D-ring bar. Align the two ends together at the halfway mark on the back as in step 2. Glue the layers together. Punch two holes for the eyelets at each end. Attach D-rings to the ends of the chain.

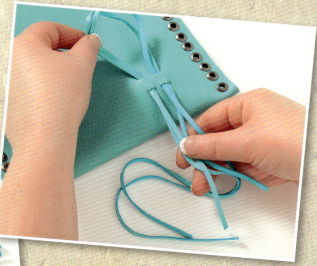

6 Cut two 13 in. (32.5 cm) lengths of lacing. Thread a pair of lacing ends through one top slit and out the bottom slit. Repeat with the other pair of ends in the other set of slits.

7 Thread a silver bead onto each pair of lacing ends and tie the lacing in a tight knot below the bead.

8 Position and mark the placement of the screw post flower in order to line up with the lacing loop. Punch a hole, through the front flap, thread in the screw post, and secure with the screw on the back.

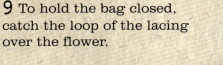

9 To hold the bag closed, catch the loop of the lacing over the flower.

rising moon

rising moon

Make these earrings in any color to match a favorite outfit—they also make a quick, easy, and unusual gift that is sure to please. Add more dangles, chain, or bead if you prefer a bolder look

1 Cut out the circles, two large in turquoise, two medium in yellow, and two small in green. Punch a small hole (see page 24) in the top and bottom of both turquoise circles. To remove any leather threads on the edges, quickly run each circle through the flame of a lighter. Don't burn the leather—you need just to touch the edge briefly with the flame.

2 Punch a hole in the top only of all the other circles. Stack a set of circles so they align at the top edge. Attach the circles together with a jump ring at the top. Attach an earring wire. Repeat with the other set of circles.

Tip: My circles were 1¼ in. (3 cm), ¾ in. (2 cm), and ⅜ in. (1 cm) in diameter, but you can make yours bigger for more dramatic earrings if you prefer.

3 Make two dangles as described on page 31 and attach to the bottom of each earring.

templates

All templates are full size, except the Buckled up strap and the
Mystical braid cuff, which need to be enlarged by 200%.

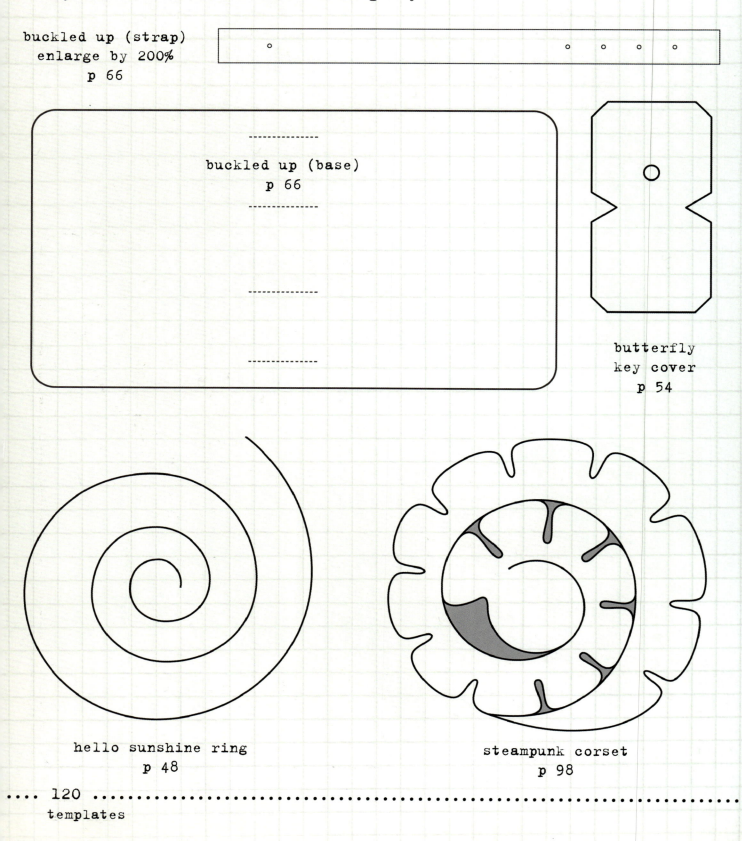

buckled up (strap)
enlarge by 200%
p 66

buckled up (base)
p 66

butterfly
key cover
p 54

hello sunshine ring
p 48

steampunk corset
p 98

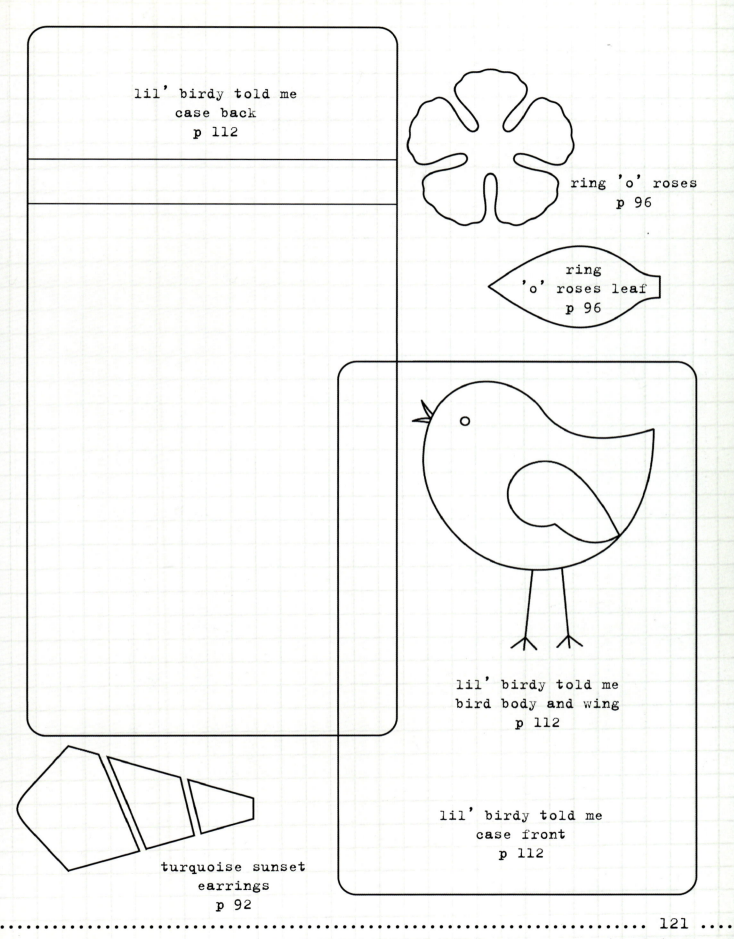

lil' birdy told me
case back
p 112

ring 'o' roses
p 96

ring
'o' roses leaf
p 96

lil' birdy told me
bird body and wing
p 112

lil' birdy told me
case front
p 112

turquoise sunset
earrings
p 92

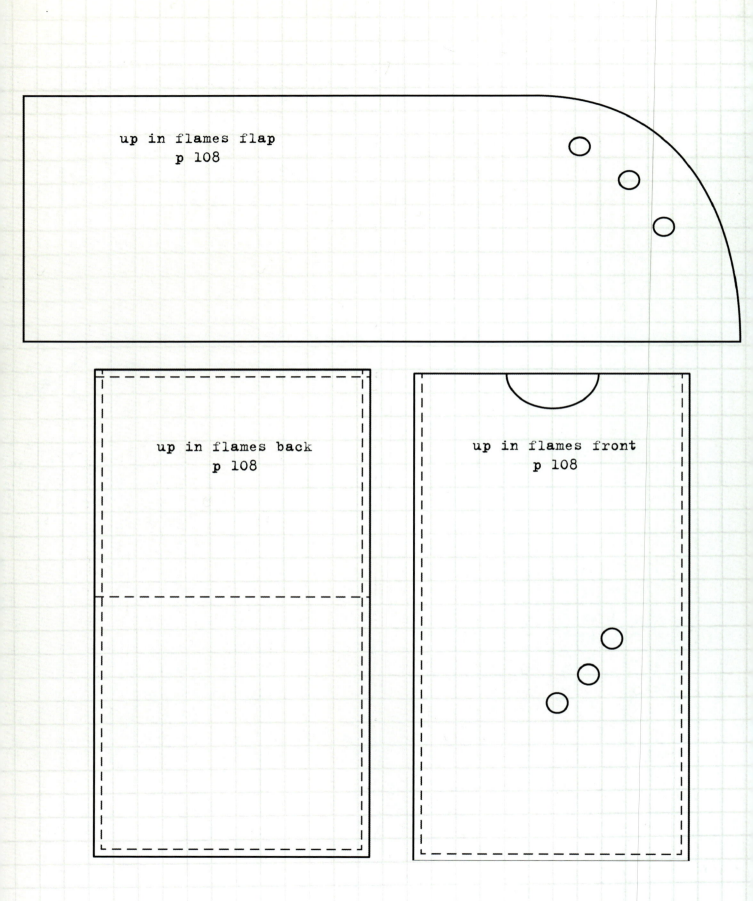

up in flames flap
p 108

up in flames back
p 108

up in flames front
p 108

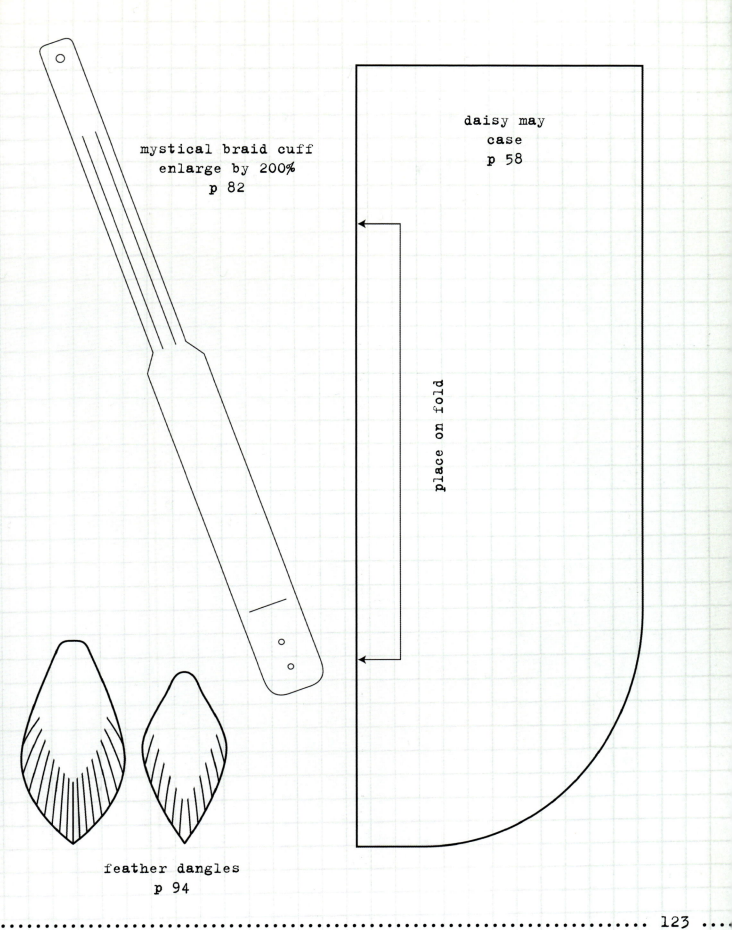

mystical braid cuff
enlarge by 200%
p 82

daisy may
case
p 58

place on fold

feather dangles
p 94

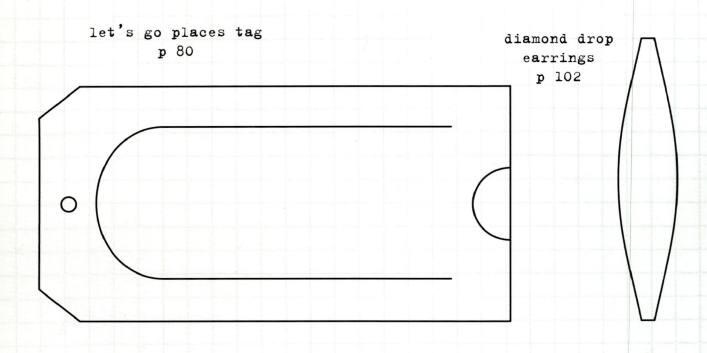

let's go places tag
p 80

diamond drop
earrings
p 102

index

resources

Linda Peterson
Website: lindapetersondesigns.com

Facebook:
Linda Molden Peterson

Twitter:
LindaPetersonTV

Youtube:
youtube.com/lindapetersondesigns

Pinterest:
Lindapet

Email:
lindapetersondesigns@yahoo.com

US SUPPLIERS

MATERIALS

Special materials used in the projects.

MD Hobby & Craft
Duckbill scissors
www.mdhobbyandcraft.com

Beadalon, Inc
Basic jewelry findings, jewelry-making
tools, small hand tools
www.beadalon.com

Ranger Inc
Alcohol-based inks
www.rangerink.com

Copic Markers
Alcohol-based markers
www.periodstyle.com

Plaid®
Acrylic paint
www.plaidonline.com

Silver Creek Leather Company
Flat laces, boho laces, round laces,
threads, general leather tools
www.silvercreekleather.com

ImpressArt
Metal stamping tools, alphabet sets
www.impressart.com

GENERAL CRAFT

Craft materials and tools.

Hobby Lobby stores
www.hobbylobby.com

Michaels stores
1800-642-4235
www.michaels.com

A.C. Moore
1-888-226-6673
www.acmoore.com

JoAnn Crafts
1-888-739-4120
www.joann.com

Springfield Leather Company
www.springfieldleather.com

UK SUPPLIERS

MATERIALS

Materials used in the projects.

The Bead Shop
Basic jewelry findings, beads, charms, jewelry-making tools
www.the-beadshop.co.uk

Artisan Leather
Leather blanks, laces, cords, decorative studs and rivets, leatherworking tools
www.artisanleather.co.uk

Bowstock Leatherworking Supplies
Leather, laces, cords, leatherworking tools
www.bowstock.co.uk

Craft Obsessions
Alcohol-based inks
www.craftobsessions.co.uk

Amazon
Alcohol-based inks and markers, stamps, punches, duckbill scissors
www.amazon.co.uk

GENERAL CRAFT

Craft materials and tools.

Hobbycraft
Stores nationwide, call 0330 026 1400
www.hobbycraft.co.uk

Crafty Devils Paper Craft
Online store
www.craftydevilspapercraft.co.uk

John Lewis
Stores nationwide
www.johnlewis.com

The Craft Barn
Online store
www.thecraftbarn.co.uk

The Range
Stores across England and online store
www.therange.co.uk

acknowledgments

Just as they say it takes a town to raise a child, it takes a great team to create a book! While I may be the name on the front cover, this book is not possible without the help of my great team: my publisher, Cindy Richards and her talented team of Sally Powell and Miriam Catley; my personal editor, Marie Clayton, who spent endless hours poring over my words; my photographer, Geoff Dann, who is brilliant at making my work shine, and his assistant, Marc Harvey; and my project stylist, Luis Peral and style photographer, Emma Mitchell. Thank you all for each of your talents and efforts into creating this book! You are the best!

Also a great big shout out to the best hand-model ever, my daughter Mariah Welsh for her patience and help in creating this book. She's really my personal assistant and I couldn't do what I do without her!

To my family, my ever-supporting husband, Dana, and kids, thank you for jumping in and getting things done while I poured my soul into this book. This is a sacrifice of love from you to me. I love you all!